MARFAN

Also by Peter Reading

Collected Poems:
1: Poems 1970-1984
(Bloodaxe Books, 1995)

Water and Waste (1970)
For the Municipality's Elderly (1974)
The Prison Cell & Barrel Mystery (1976)
Nothing For Anyone (1977)
Fiction (1979)
Tom o' Bedlam's Beauties (1981)
Diplopic (1983)
5x5x5x5x5 (1983)
C (1984)

Collected Poems:
2: Poems 1985-1996
(Bloodaxe Books, 1996)

Ukulele Music (1985)
Going On (1985)
Stet (1986)
Final Demands (1988)
Perduta Gente (1989)
Shitheads (1989)
Evagatory (1992)
Last Poems (1994)
Eschatological (1996)

Work in Regress (Bloodaxe Books, 1997)
Ob. (Bloodaxe Books, 1999)

MARFAN

Peter Reading

with photographs by
JAY SHUTTLEWORTH

BLOODAXE BOOKS

ISBN: 1 85224 516 6

First published 2000 by
Bloodaxe Books Ltd,
P.O. Box 1SN,
Newcastle upon Tyne NE99 1SN.

Bloodaxe Books Ltd acknowledges
the financial assistance of Northern Arts.

Peter Reading wishes to thank the Lannan Foundation
for their Literary Residency in Texas in 1998-99.

Cover printing by J. Thomson Colour Printers Ltd, Glasgow.

Printed in Great Britain by
Cromwell Press Ltd, Trowbridge, Wiltshire.

To Deborah Reading

Look eastward from the back porch in late June:

Venus ascends, one hour before the Sun,
over the water tower (which fecund belly
sustains this drouth-town's viability).

'Aint none knows whar she come from, o whar shays goin.'

'Jus rides that *burro* roun from place to place.'

'Ya sees her whan yer least expectin it...'

The Burro Lady ties her moke to a post
at Chuy's (now defunct) Mexican Diner
and goes for coffee into Dairy Queen.

She has the *frisson*-fright air of a gypsy –
gaudily-coloured wrap-rounds, plastic flip-flops
with spurs incongruously fixed at the heels.

The *burro*, draped with saddle-bags and blankets,
is pale, pale, pale, pale, in this evening's light.

I don't know what they signify, but it's scary.

Reading in Marfa Public Library:
Qui Caecus et Senectute Confectus.

Across an arid, silent scrubland blackness
the raucous trumpet hails the malfortunates...

Night, Union Pacific freight trains braying
lullaby them to sleep: ˘ — | ˘ —

Approaching D (*allegro moderato*).

One evening, back in 1883,
Robert Reed Ellison was with his wife
herding a bunch of cattle across the basin
from Alpine towards Marfa, heading west,
and, sundown coming on, stopped for the night.
As he made preparations for the campfire
he glanced up and was mystified to notice
lights flickering to and fro across a valley
along the side of the Chinati Mountains.
Assuming it was Apaches on the move,
he catnapped clutching his Winchester till dawn
when the weird incandescence fizzled out.

A short time after that, a young surveyor,
man by the name of Williams, was out mapping
round the same spot and saw the same strange lights.
His journal records how 'Indians of this region
believe the luminosity to be
the restless spirit of the dead Apache,
Chief Alsate.'

                 Nearly a century later,
the *Houston Chronicle* despatched Stan Redding –
'Check out this Marfa story; let's just see
whether there's anything in it.' As he drove

along a dirt road near Paisano Pass,
Redding observed the Marfa Mystery Lights:
They darted about the ground – red, white and blue,
orbs, baseball-sized. They blended into one,
then separated. One of them would zoom
high in the air, then plummet into the brush,
then rise an instant later and spin away
crazily. Unsupported and unattached,
each one illuminated the black-brush clump
over which it hovered.

                    Tonight, off 90 East,
a curious *ignis fatuus* fulminates...

[Some feller driving a Chevrolet pickup truck
gave me a ride from Alpine on East 90,
and, as we motored, confided this to me:]

Ya know, thay stop me sometimes, tham thar cops,
and take me downtown with'm tew thar **station.**
Thay thay thay thay thay make me do tham **tests.**
Thay say ah done a **wrong thang,** *but ah never.*
Thay say mah wrists got someways sort of **gashed.**
Thay say people like me is goddam **pests.**
Thay thay thay thay thay found me in a drain
and sent me to that **Rehabilitation**
Center *(that's whar thay send ya whan ya* **trashed),**
thay gev ya coffee thar and feed ya slops...

[Then let you out to *integrate* again
and makeshift to the best of your endeavour.]

The dress and souvenir shop on the corner
was formerly Kerrs' Filling Station – back
in 1920, Arthur, Orr and Klyde
Kerr purveyed Fords, served gas and were mechanics
for the few cars in Marfa, and they supplied
kerosene for folks' lamps.

                The brothers Kerr
sold W.H. Cleveland, a local rancher,
a Model T. They showed him how to start it,
which process Cleveland grasped, but they neglected
to demonstrate how he should stop the thing.

He scorched off to his ranch, yelled the day's orders
to his cowhands, U-turned and headed back
to Marfa.

          Circling round and round and round
in front of Kerrs' he hollered '*WHOA THAR, HOSS!*'
repeatedly until one of the brothers
leapt on the running-board, roped in the critter,
and skidded it adroitly to submission
swathed in a cloud of Southwest Texas dust.

The depositional Marfa Basin formed
during the Permian (which began about

280,000,000 years ago
and lasted about 55,000,000 years) –
a shallow, bowl-like sea where sediments
accumulated (and where we now walk,
perpetuating the depositional trait).

A Union Pacific freight train hurtles
through the night town; at each street intersection
(bells, red lights, semaphore of barber-pole
barriers) the engineer hits the hooter –
a raucous howl, audible for five miles
across the silent, arid scrubland basin
where, in a blackness, some malfortunate
is woken by the cacophonic trumpet,
listens, and ruminates, and fears the dark.

Tonight's anxieties: a labial lump;
pain in the kidneys and the abdomen;
and money, money, money, money, money.

where maledicts are shivering in the pit
though scorching heat is unassuaged   where breath
exhaled is woeful   where black corvids scavenge

A solitary, voluntary exile
respires hot, fan-rotated desert air
in a southwestern public library.

where they lie sullen in black slurry   where
powerless to speak they gurgle disregarded
where dolorous groans begin   where plangent wails
of lamentation sickeningly arise
where no light penetrates   where Stygian squalls
thrash every victim equal   desperate shrieks
and supplicant imprecations are ignored

The final over; everyone is out.

The Classics shelf in Marfa Public Library:
incongruously stuffed between two volumes
of the *Commedia*, a tattered *Wisden*
charts the achievements of that English summer
before climacteric and post bellum slump.

The Mourning Dove bag should be good round Marfa;
meanwhile, the telly chirpily reports
it's Open Season on the kids in Baghdad.

Wine from Fort Stockton; sunset; Chinese poem.

I blow the Chihuahuan dust from his *Collected*.
Ewart is three-years-dead; this is the desert.

A roadside Turkey Vulture scrutinises
the hesitant progress of a passer-by.

The First Episcopal Church of Holy Shit
clanks its complacent bell across the basin.

Even the *Big Bend Sentinel*, each week
conveys them mercilessly down the Rio –
Hernandez, Martinez, Garcia, Lopez…

We are applying *Nature's Miracle*
unto the furnishings we have besmirched.

Fuentes, Vega, Valverde, Rivera,
Morales, Flores, *descanse en paz*.

Beyond my caring and my comprehension.

We term it Marfa, but we mean the lot.

Across the windswept, Pronghorn-browsed brown grass
Judd's row of concrete, seven-foot-high boxes
stretches a mile north-south, signifies zilch.

Some days I've seen *Antilocapras* shelter
from noon sun of a hundred-and-some degrees
in those cute sculptures – yes, and shit in'm too.

Last night the snow began. At 4 this morning
the flakes are flinty, seem to shrink the face.
The walk down Washington from North Plateau –
2 inches of parochial Amundsen.

A fellow Lone Star drinker in Ray's Bar:
'Whan ya git old ya can't remember a fuck.'

Look west, beyond the Mexican Cemetery,
the Rothko Sunset and oblivion.

A CD, placed incongrously in Marfa:
Georg Philipp Telemann, who understood,
among so many other important issues,
the order of obeying descending scales.

The Baptists are in confident full cry –
their happy howls and yelps sweal from the window
of a charming little breeze-block tabernacle
and rise to join the welter of emissions
from the industrial plants both sides the border
conspiring to occlude the clear-sightedness
of those who live in Big Bend.

                             Crossing 90,
observe, above the Thunderbird Motel,
how all the shit belched skywards contributes
to the beauty of this monumental Sunset.

El Paso Airport, the Departure Lounge,
beyond the Baggage Check, beyond the Gate,
beyond the Terminal and the Rio Grande,
Mark Rothko strata grade from blood to black.

Sunset is like a busted-up fried egg.

No; like an addled egg, with drops of *sangre*.

'We love it here!', expressive of ennui.

The last ebb, the dead shingle – Marfa Basin.

The Wisdom of West Texas, a slim vol.

When this gets published I shall have to be
beyond the City Limit on a Greyhound.

For I am catapulted to the grandeur
of Marfan Literary Resident
(sinecure recently inaugurated
by the beneficence of Patrick Lannan –
blessandpreservehimandhiswholeFoundation).

Their countree doe poffefs an myriad temples:
Papifts, Epifcopalians, Methodifts,
Cowboys for Chrift, and ye Jehovah's Witnefs...
Truly a fere, yet pious, wildernefs.

The ftimulus of ftrong drink is oft required.

'Twas then they sent in Lannan's Secret Weapon.

From the Mexican: The Sun unfoldeth pink
on peaks across the Rio Bravo – ridge
on ridge on ridge on ridge on ridge on ridge...
and I am exiled in El Paso Airport
while my belovèd flyeth; yet the Sun
riseth, illuminateth – is this hope?

The artist Donald Judd deigned to descend
here in the 1970s, and proceeded
(courtesy of vast funding from his patron)
to launch himself indulgently upon
a spoilt-child, hedonistic shopping-spree
procuring half the town.

                    In '79,
to gratify a yen to establish plush
permanent installations of his own
and of his buddies' bourgeois artefacts,
he bought the army camp, or, as he writes
with characteristic magnanimity
and not a little chutzpah: 'I agreed
to have the Dia Foundation come to Marfa
and purchase the main buildings and the land
of Fort D.A. Russell, on the edge of town.'

That's where he housed his famous magnum opus –
one hundred waist-high milled aluminium boxes
betokening genius spawned of privilege.

Manifestly possessed of major talent,
what ingenious *kunstwerke* would he have, perforce,
produced if big-money backers had been absent
to finance these billion-dollar, minimalist,
factory-finish, self-indulgent art games?

In Judd's *Collected Writins* he says, I'm tole:
'I have a complex on a city block
in Marfa, Texas, between Highway 90
and the Southern Pacific Railroad Company track
next to a cattlefeed mill, *unfortunately*' –
he'd bought the place in the early '70s
an found he couldn't git tew sleep o'nights
because of th'honest noise of manufacture.

Now Godbold's mill was established back in May
of 1946 when 'Happy' Roy Godbold
bought the feed business off'n ol' Harper Rawlings –
the name thay gev it wus 'Ranchers' Feed & Supplies'.
Seems to me carpetbaggers shouldn't complain.

The Marfan Bourgeois with their *Howdy, Peter!*s...
After about a dozen Margaritas
I puke and say how cute their 3-piece suite is.

[The Chevy driver is on red alert:]

Ya know thay got this television disc
outside mah neighbor's cabin but thay don't know
ah know it's not for satellite TV
but that thay got it pointing right inside
mah head the CIA tew find out what
ah think about tham beamed encrypted signals
transmitted from the Godbold's feedmill silo
beaming mah brains up tew the President
who sent the US Navy into town
tew place electric wiring between me
and the Presidio County Courthouse statue
which prickly pears transmits it tew the White House
out of the desert whan the Pentagon
will tell me that that that the President
that that that that that handgun that that that

Presidio County Courthouse, Marfa, built
in 1886 of native stone
and bricks made locally, three storeys high
with an octagonal tower capped by a dome
on top of which the fancy classical figure
of Justice once held in her outstretched digits
the symbol of her calling but now fingers
only the dusty hot air off the desert –
an irate cowpoke back in history,
quitting the calaboose across the street
(where he'd been held for being drunk), observed
'There *ain't* no justice in this goddam county',
and shot the scales plumb out of the goddess's hand.

Stone calaboose, built 1886
but now redundant, used for archiving
paperwork from the County Sheriff's office;

foot-thick steel door; a steel-grilled fenestration;
torn scribbled notice **JAiLeR WiLL HAnd oUT rAZORs
To gET A rAZEr YoU MUSt HAnD OnE iN**;

the 'Old Cage' dumped nostalgically out front,
incorporating four fold-down steel bunks
within the cramped cold ferric lattice trap.

To the Editor, the *Big Bend Sentinel* –
Sir, I was on 90, Marfa to Alpine,
when a white sport utility vehicle came
right up behind and passed me pretty quick.

My Cruise Control was set at 70
(the legal limit in Presidio County).

I couldn't help but notice that on the rear
license plate was inscribed the following
in fancy letters: **Texas County Judge**.

Ah holed up with a bunch of Peccaries
[*Tayassu tajacu*], tham Javelinas.

Ah'd fell out with the wife an drank some Lone Stars,
than, thar in that Fort D.A. Russell outfit,
ya know, whar thay got all tham Artist Judds?,
ah seen em headin into the ventilation
gap of a beat-up hut as ain't been touched
since 1946 or tharabouts.

Wall, what'd ah do but foller em right in thar –
a big ol' boar about a meter long,
four females an a couple o' young uns, yaller,
with black stripes down thar backs, an thar thay lay.

O' course the ol' male grunted an barked a whiles,
but ah jus crep thar, mong the shit an cobwebs,
an soon thay all jus fell asleep – it's hot, see?,
bout over a hundred in the middle day
(normly, thay'd be in Prickly Pear or brush).

Wall, ah wus thar for bout two hours, an than
thay high-tailed, doin Peccary stuff, ah guess.

The *fons et origo*, El Cheapo Liquor,
good Mescal with its fat worm in the lees,
Agave, armed with teeth like a goddam shark.

It's Xenophobia, but pretends to be
outraged concern that hundreds of tons of drugs
are flooding across the Mexico/US line
each year – the hatred's in the stupid faces,
the stupid quasi-military duds,
the stupid guns of off-duty Patrolmen
in Carmen's stuffing their porcine guts with shite
before resuming the cat-and-mouse charade
of rounding up the smooth-faced, terrified *hijos*,
viejas, *campesinos* cowered in scrub
this side the Rio Grande...

                              Washington:
congressional Republicans are baying
for bigger fences, more technology,
more agents and the US military
to stem the tide; the House of Representatives
is calling for 10,000 soldiers to guard
2,000 miles of US/Mexican frontier,
elaborate triple-fencing barriers
(*especially whar tham mothers tries to crass
from Juárez to El Paso*), and an entire
new agency for borderline enforcement
(*our border's a national secur'ty threat,
and bah God, sah!, bah God, sah!, Congress better
start a-securin-of our border, pronto!*).
The Senate is considering these demands
together with one to add 5,000 more
Border Patrol Gestapo and to provide
sophisticated high-tech apparatus
for the fat, trigger-happy, complacent twats.

shooting of teen-age boy

...ed in border

13. viii. 98
Big Bend Sentinel

Sixteen new Border Patrol recruits were sworn in Monday as the agency increases its presence here.

Peter Reading
2. ix. 98.

[The Mystery Lights, the *ignis fatuus*
that hurteth not, but only feareth fooles,
elucidated by the Chevy driver:]

Ya know, tham lights back thar on 90 East,
thays flickerin signal messages tew me
most every night straight from the CIA,
thay thay thay thay thay thay thay thay thay thay
thay say thay say   ah keep mah handgun loaded

In January 1881,
work on the Galveston/San Antonio
Southern Pacific Railroads reached this site,
a water stop and freight headquarters which, then,
had no name. Southern Pacific's Engineer
was married to a woman who aspired
to *higher things* (was reading Dostoevski,
The Brothers Karamazov, 1880);
she dubbed the tank town Marfa, after the loyal
retainer of the Karamazov household,
omniscient old Marfa Ignatyevna
who did not see the fall but heard the scream,
the strange, foam-stifled, long familiar scream
of an epileptic falling in a fit.

The Lights, demystified by divers eminents:
electrostatic discharge; swamp-gas; moonlight
shining on veins of mica; ghosts of Spanish

Conquistadors who sought gold here; a mirage
produced by cold and hot layers of air
refracting light; *Ya know tham Mystery Flickers?,*
well, what it is, the CIA is beaming
encrypted messages from Washington
onto the water tower – ya know, that silver
cylinder thar with MARFA writ on?, well,
tham coded signals bounce right off the tower
and light up the entire Chinati Mountains
with flicker flicker flicker flicker flicker

US 90 East, Marfa to Alpine:
you drive through the volcano of Paisano –
just breccia 35 million years old,
caldera, and pale rhyolite, and you.

No-nuke groups lobby governor to resist
proposals for Sierra Blanca site.
(Headline in this week's *Big Bend Sentinel*.)

Sierra Blanca residents have voiced
concern over the Texas, Maine and Vermont
Compact, which would enable the three states
to dump low-level radioactive shit
on an impoverished minority's doorstep,
in violation of the federal
and international environmental
agreements made between the USA
and Mexico.

It doesn't matter though –
they're only Spiks out on the borderline
(a site beneath which lie tectonic faults
rendering it more seismically active
than any other in the Lone Star State).

Outside the Mexican Cemetery, a sign
to visitors is crackling and buckled
from solar blistering over generations
and winds sand-blasted off the Chihuahuan Desert:
$200 FINE FOR LOITERING
OR LITTERING HERE.

                              In this place idlers throng;
discarded stones, wood crosses, painted plaster,
and plastic roses faded to pinkish grey
garbage the quiet, death-sustaining slope.

Morales, Marquez, Garcia, Martinez,
Flores, Rivera, Hinojos-Hernandez…

Spiked on a Yucca sprouting from the dirt
of Maria Bartolo Villanueva,
a straw-stuffed rag doll, smiling, rosy-cheeked,
sporting a hat of bean-sack hessian –
the pious tribute of some *hijo*.

                              Coveys
of Scaled Quail loiter, litter among the ash,
scutter a dusty plot where Moniga
Quinteros de Salgado is reposing,
churr a low nasal *Descanse en Paz*.

The bails are scattered, the last man run out.

Wisden recalls the English ignominy…
A solitary, voluntary exile
respires hot, fan-rotated desert air
in a southwestern public library.

$10 in advance! The Marfa Lights
Festival (held on Labor Day Weekend)!
This year we feature the great Dana Lee
& Mariachi de la Paz of Alpine;
the one and only Shelly Lares – enjoy!
[Also, a bunch of other total shites
like 'Randy' Bob Pulido ('Texas Cowboy');
and, all the way from Marfa, 'Injun Dancers';
'Los City Boyz'…] **And, don't forget, at 9,**
the 3-on-3 Hoop-D-Do Street Basketball
Tournament – remember, y'all come and see…
[some banjo-pluckin' strumpet from Big Bend –
all in all, a load of fucking chancers.]
Way wish a Texas 'Howdy!' tew y'all!

The Editor, the *Big Bend Sentinel* – Sir,
Miguel de la Madrid and Ronald Reagan
agreed the Treaty of 1983,
protecting a zone 60 miles either side
the US/Mexico border, and committing
each government to turn down any project
that could affect the other's side of the line.

In 1998 the US House
of Representatives agreed a measure
allowing Maine and Vermont to ship low-level
radioactive waste to this proposed
site (which lies 20 miles from Mexican soil),
in exchange for which those two states would pay out
$25,000,000 (each) to Texas.

An old-timer in Ray's Bar told me how,
during the Great Depression of '33,
he'd 'rid the parallel truss-bars underneath
a boxcar of the Southern Pacific freight'.
I put another Lone Star on the tab
and he expatiated:

       Tham wus the days
whan one in five wus jobless an headin West.
Ya'd grip the iron truss-rods used to strenthen
the railroad cars – ya'd only be ten inches
off'n the rails. The trick wus gettin a board
an layin it across the horizontal
rods, so's ya'd hev a kinda shelf to lay on
face down, eyes closed against the flyin dirt
as blowed up off'n the track.

       A frenna mine

nodded asleep, rolled off, an skrithered along
under the wheels like butcher meat.

                              We flipped
the freights, we ditched the bulls, we decked the rattlers
an rid the rods. Thay called us bums an bos
an yeggs, an now it seems a long ways back...
Whan ya git old ya can't remember shit.

Encrypted – thars a word the CIA
uses tew mean thar sendin me in code
the latest information from the White House.
Thay sends it different ways. The Burro Lady
(ya know, the lady travels all around
by mule, folk say she carries all her things
on that thar burro, everythin she owns,
she even goes as far as Marathon
sleepin along the highway, all her stuff
just danglin off the burro, pots an pans
an raggy clothes an stuff, strapped on the mule,
ya see her sleepin trussed up like a bundle
smack by the highway), well, she oftentimes
signals tew me as she goes ridin by –
thay comes from Washington, tham signals, coded,
but mah ole Chevy here [he pats the dashboard]
decodes tham ole encrypteds, every one.

The indigenous salutation, *How y'all?*,
induces, when the first *frisson* of the drawl
wears off, a desire to puke against a wall,
or evacuate one's chitterling, or spawl.

Hawthorne in Marfa Public Library:

I sailed on the 'Niagara' out of Boston,
saluted by the guns on Castle Island,
to Liverpool in '53. But now
I miss my hillside and my pen. The British,
sodden in strong beer, have a conversation
like a plum pudding – stodgy, bilious.

El Paisano Hotel, corner of Highland,
completed 1930, designed by Trost
& Trost, El Paso, in grand quasi-Spanish
Baroque style, built around a central courtyard
with fountain, ornate, long ago fucked up.

In '55 they made the movie *Giant*
in these parts and the crew and cast put up
at El Paisano – in the now musty lobby
autographed fading snaps of quondam stars
(Rock Hudson, Jimmy Dean, Elizabeth Taylor...)
embellish the dirty yellow walls, alongside
the scruffy mop-heads of a Texas Longhorn
and a Bison (Bisons were extirpated here,

along with Indians, by about 1880).

The cobwebbed photo of a prize Hereford bull,
immortalised in 1950, when
he won the American Royal Show in Kansas,
testifies to his having been called Jug,
bred up by ol' man Mitchell's sons from Marfa.

[An old-timer in Ray's Bar told me how:]
Bout three, four years ago we wus called out
to just this side of Van Horn here on 90 –
Union Pacific'd gotten itself derailed.
State Troopers wus all thar as well as us
Fire Service critters, plus a buncha boys
out'n the Sheriff's Office.

                            Wayl, that wreck
really wus somethin – nobody wus hurt
but one tham freight trucks had been fulla brandy
an busted open. We fetched a fire truck full
back into town, an Sheriff an the Troopers
didn't go short I guess. I still got three
full gallon bottles a-waitin thar back home.

In '36 the Hotel building housed:
Bledsoe & Swearingem [I swear it!], Lawyers;
and W.B. Mitchell & Sons, Ranchers...
Hal Trost's anachronistic Baroque folly,
built for an oil boom that did not transpire.

Zane Grey, the author of Westerns, came to Marfa
a couple of times, researching for his book
The Lone Star Ranger, which he dedicated
to Jeff Vaughan – Ranger, Deputy U.S. Marshal,
Customs Official, Sheriff of Presidio,
served as a judge in the World Series Rodeo
at Madison Square Garden, N.Y. City.
Vaughan had a horse called Jack o' Diamonds, raised
on the Bite Ranch and famous for his style
and custom-crafted saddle with hand carvings
and fancy silver ornamental tooling.

Some feller I met in Ray's Bar told me how
one night, after a dozen or so Lone Stars,
as he was going for home, he saw Jeff Vaughan
on Jack o' Diamonds and Zane Grey on a *burro*
heading down Highland from the County Courthouse.
He mumbled 'How y'all?' and they said 'Howdy',
then rode, transparent, plumb through the Library wall.

Three locos, hundred-seventeen freight-cars,
discordant mile-long Union Pacific howl.

Editor:
I notice that Mr. Jeff Hubbard, in one of his Honest, Competent and Qualified advertisements for himself (Big Bend Sentinel, 10.15.98), perpetuates the solecism "miniscule" where minuscule is the mot juste.

Peter Reading
Marfa

CUNT TWIRLY

The Big Bend Sentinel, Marfa, Texas, October 2, 1998

Jeff Hubbard for County Judge

Presidio County

Jeff

Hubbard

for

County Judge

Honest, Competent and Qualified

...my objective is to protect private property & ... landowners of this ... ... rather than t... ...way to rape the ...

vote for **Jeff Hub**...

...ward for County Judge.

CUNT TWIRLY

To the Editor, the *Big Bend Sentinel* –
Late Saturday night some hoodlum element
daubed orange paint graffiti on several signs
which picture the prospective Candidate
for County Judge in the forthcoming poll,
Mr Jeff Hubbard. ['Twirly', our sobriquet,
occasioned by his brash mustachio.]
Scrawling such things is bad enough itself,
but when you realise that some of these
words by the 'midnight artists' are the most
dirty, obscene and blasphemous on earth,
it is intolerable! One of the signs
happens to be on 90 next to El Cheapo,
directly opposite the Catholic Church.
[Some wag had sprayed **CUNT TWIRLY** on the placard.]
Can you imagine what parishioners thought
when they drove in for Mass on Sunday morning?

Tham Marfa Lahbry folks tole may Zahn Grah
dahd Altadena, Californahyay,
bout nahnteen tharty nahn – s hah come that dude
in Ray's rickns hay seenm jis lays nah
on Hahlan rahdn a motherfucker *burro*?

The fins no longer spinning on the mast
of the Aermotor Windmill Company pump;
the circular, concrete-lined, brick water-tank
empty, dead *Corvus corax* in its dregs;

the ranch-house harbouring dead Horned Lizards, parched;
the shelf where a deceased Dude Rancher's Mescal,
half full, supports its fat worm in the lees…

You and I swig it, Johnston, and growl 'Cheers'
to the Old Boy who went stiff four years back.

A lone vexed longhorn bull, malevolent,
rattles the rotting, tied-together rails
round the corral, built about 1920
by the Galveston, Harrisburg & San Anton'
Rail Company. These defunct stockpens served
a central shipping point for animals raised
in Brewster, Presidio and Jeff Davis Counties.

As many as 70,000 head of cattle
were shipped from these yards in a single year.

Pens were enlarged in 1929
to handle the extraordinary expansion
of business.

By the '30s sheep and goats
were also being lugged from here. The trade
declined some after trucking was introduced.

The Stockyards are still used to weigh beasts prior
to shipment:

RAILROAD PENS, OWNED/OPERATED
BY FOWLKES'S CATTLE Co. (INCORPORATED)
RECEIVING STOCK 8 t' 3 WEDNSDAYS

OR BY REQQST. FER ALL Yr TRUCKIN nEEDS.

A remedy for all that is not good:
Mezcal (also to celebrate good things).

(**Hubbard's opponent romps to victory** –
headline in this week's *Big Bend Sentinel*.)

Poor Twirly, pompous, puffed, opinionated,
yet, as the poll discloses clearly, hated.

On Highway 385 out of Fort Stockton,
going through Marathon to Persimmon Gap,
you are following the Great Comanche War Trail.

The savages drifted south into the Big Bend
during the 1840s-1880s
to raid *our* ranches, settlements, wagon trains,
both sides the Rio Grande.

                         Five miles south
of Marathon, Fort Pena Colorado
was built in '79 to nail the redskins.

The Southern Pacific Railroad Company
got here in '81, supplying the Fort
and ranches with essential guns and stores.

Since the Comanche has been extirpated
things hereabouts have been just hunky-dory –
the Chisos Gallery vends Ranch Antiques,
and Nicely Restored Cottages are for rent.

Wayl, ah woke up thays mornin kinda ahly,
sun wus jus rahzn over the water tower
makin it look pinksilver, kinda purdy.

Wayl, ah wus spose bay warkn foh ol Fowlkes
over the Cattle Pens, s ah tuke the Chev
an gt thar bout, oh, aytah clock ah gays.

Wayl, Longhorn bull in thah, bayn thah ahl nah,
purdy dam mean, hay hollered at may ten times –

wayl, the tenth letter of th alphybayt
is J, an, since mah naym is Jeremiah,
ah figure as hays atryin tew contac may
concernin sumptn from the CIA.

The crumbling tomb of Señora Prieto
piously venerated with a posy
of plastic roses in a Bud Light empty.

On 90 East from Marfa through to Alpine
a section of dense brush, low oaks and thorns
harbours Wild Turkeys. A covey of 15
females flaps heavily against driving rain
over the Chev, just clearing it by inches.
When I get home I'll fax this to you, Johnston,
then drain a 6 of Michelob in their honour.

Morning. Above this arid scrubland basin,
three dozen Sandhill Cranes, at about a thousand
feet, circle, bugle-croaking, south. Late Fall.

Presidio County Courthouse: on the Green,
a disgorged pellet of *Sylvilagus* bones;
above, in a long-established Cottonwood,
the privilege of a Great Horned Owl at roost.

[The quarterly *Desert Candle* carries this
story of a **West Texas Visitation**:]

Week before Christmas, 1996.
Juanita in her kitchen at Fort Stockton,
making tortillas for her family's dinner,
her mind not on the meal but on her son
(died in the line of Border Patrol duty
some years before) and of how terribly lonely
Christmas would be without him.

                              When she sat
at table with her family ready to eat,
she served a few tortillas and then noticed
one in particular – 'When I went to eat it,
I saw the donkey! I saw the ears and head,
and then the legs, and then I saw the Virgin
Mary riding, holding the Baby Jesus!'

It seemed to her that even in West Texas
Jesus comes visiting sometimes, that in this
Blessèd Tortilla was writ the Word of God.
So she has kept this epiphanous tortilla,
which lightened the burthen of her grief somewhat,
and has it still.

                  When, recently, in Alpine,
the *Desert Candle* made a photocopy
of the tortilla, the contrast in the print
clarified the image enough to see –
well, look for yourselves, examine the tortilla:
the *burro*, Mary, Jesus AND JOSEPH TOO!

DESERT CANDLE
MARFA

she saw the Virgin on the tortilla.

donkey.

A photocopy of the tortilla on which appeared, the week before Christmas 1996, this image of Mary, holding the Baby Jesus, riding on a donkey, with Joseph taking up the rear.

"somehow I didn't have the courage to eat it."

Peter Reading
18 · X · 98

Every few hundred yards they dug a culvert
beneath the Southern Pacific line (in case
floodwater rose and flashed the track away),
and under one of these (just three feet high,
two beams with sleepers across them, rails exposed)
I lay down as four Union locos, linked,
howled a two-miler, hundred-twenty trucks,
like an infuriated Mastodon
above my head – the usual P & O,
Evergreen, N.O.L., Conco and Hanjin
containers, double-stacked, clattering over...

Scared myself shitless down there; quite amusing.

[From the Chinese in Marfa Library:]

The confidence of being unobserved
induces the bored poet to pick his nose.

You too can own a bloody plastic Jesus –
$5 down the Ave Maria Gift Shop.

'Undocumented Aliens' thay call em,
tham Spiks the Border Patrol nabbed yeastarday.

When Cabeza de Vaca crossed Big Bend
in 1535 these mortar-holes
in the Cretaceous limestone riverbank shelves,
cylindrical deep metates used for grinding
grain or mesquite beans, were already ancient.

It is not known what tribe, or if they lived
under these smoke-blacked sheer precipitous cliffs,
but that each time they pestled seed or legumes
their negative memorials deepened some.

Past Boulder Meadow the trail begins to switchback
up the South Wall. Beneath the peak it passes
between a stand of Bigtooth Maples. You drop
into Boot Canyon, residual Arcady,
after the heady crest of Pinnacles,
eroded stacks, and Pinyon, Juniper, Oak,
sheer steeps down near 8,000 feet below.
From Emory you see clear to Davis Mountains,
Marfa and Alpine and a hundred miles
into the smog of hapless Mexico.

Kickoff, the Shorthorns' great Homecoming game;
the martial clangor and the menacing drum;
they look like extras out of *Ivanhoe* –
bright helmets, visors, armoured shoulders, greaves,
tensed ready for the Tourney and the Tilt
in the grim Lists at Ashby-de-la-Zouch.

In Hicksville, real estate is snapped up – arties,
architects, carpet-baggers, entrepreneurs,
'gallery owners', leather coat boutiquesters...

The indigenous can fuck off outa here.

Lit by a horizontal sunrise shaft,
a Golden Eagle gleams from the highest perch
of that tall conifer across the street,
corner of Washington and North Plateau.
About this there is no more to be written.

Ah have mah copy of this month's *Christian Ranchman*
right heah, Cowboys foh Chras, ah thank y'all!,
an, bah the grace of God, ah know ahm saved!

Ah like thas cowboy styla preachin – how
ya finish ya devotions foh the day
with a bo-dacious buck off. But the hahlight
is knowin ya do God's work bah leadin folks
tew Jesus. Jesus heals tham who is hooked
on drink an rescues many, many souls!

Ah see an ad. heah foh a Guardian Angel
in gold or silver, wearin a stetson, jus
4 bucks – wayl ahl bay hog-tied; sen may wone!

Ah see wone heah foh Cowboys foh Chras belt-buckles
in antique bronze or silver with gold inlay,
sayn 'COWBOYS FOH CHRAS' an 'JESUS CHRAS IS LOWD'
writ thah right own the thayng – 35 bucks.

Ah see a testimowny framma sinna
whew foun God's Glory – it's a Glory Story!

An nah ah wans tew say a leel ol prar:

Ah bin a cowpoke, Lowd, a long tahm, it seems,
aworkin an adreamin cowpoke dreams.

But lately, thars ahankerin in mah soul
foh tew git mahself rah unner Yoh control!

So, with mah spurs an chaps an hat in haynd,
ahm headin, with ol Blu, foh the Promiss Laynd.

Now thars a light in Hayvn ahm longn tew see
an ah heah Jesus calln – yep, foh me!

Some loophole in the system here allows
the region's oldest industries to dodge
state air pollution legal regulations –
older facilities are not obliged,
if they were built prior to '71,
to meet the Texas Clean Air Act requirements
that 'best available control technologies'
be used. They were excluded, or 'Grandfathered',
from any newer, more exacting laws.
Grandfathered industries around the region
emit the same nitrogen oxide levels
as about 3 million motor cars, while coal-powered
Mexican Carbon I & II plants belch
more than 250,000 tons
of sulphur dioxide yearly into the mild
south-easterly breeze, which wafts it sweetly over
the Big Bend National Park and fucks it good.

Th BP boys is doin wayl agin –
th Marfa Sector pulled in three more on em,
Undocumented Spiks lookin fer wk.

[Headline in this week's *Big Bend Sentinel*:
Marfa hosts international architects.]

'The concrete used in the Marfa sewer plant
is just the same as Judd used in his pieces.
That shows that it is not the thing you use
but what you do with it,' explains Alexacos.

'This town is how it look because the buildings,'
Hazin Anuar is hasty to opine.

'I walk into a garage and I talk
happily to the owner,' says Onishi.
'If I do that in London, he have say
"Why, please, will you not quickly go away!"'

A newly dug up ancient Indian campfire,
this side of Alpine, was discovered when
the city sewer line was being surveyed.
The basin-shaped, intact Native American
hearth was revealed, 3 feet diameter,
placed in a shallow excavated pit,
constructed with vesicular laval basalt
and other cobbles. Charcoal fragments from it
were radiocarbon dated to the time
(during the Late Archaic, over here)
when the Nazarene was hammered to his tree.

[Someone I met in Ray's Bar cornered me:]

Ya know that Ol Cage next th Calaboose,
criss-cross black steel an kinda cubic-like,
7 by 7 foot by 7 foot,
with fold-dahn bunk-bayds one above th other
2 on each side (Sheriff ud lock ya in
t sober up, years back)? Wahl, me an Lopez
(ya know, the feller as busted Sharky's nose?),
wahd hayd a few too many Lone Stars, mebbie,
an moseyed that direction goin home,
an, bein overcowm with the fatigues,
layd dahn awhiles t sooth tham fevered brows
right thar on tham ol i-ron foldin bayds.

Slep thar all night an, risin aroun noon,
moseyed dahn t El Cheapo liquor store –
git us a 6 of Lones t take the cure.

It's Big-Time Art and small-town politics.

It's the *Highest Golf-Course in the Lone Star State*
(kept verdant by the lowest water table).

To the Editor, the *Desert Candle* – Sir,
your article concerning the tortilla
with revelatory powers was no big deal.
I have at home: a partially cooked chupatti
showing a living likeness of the Buddha;
great Krishna limned in a popadam; a nacho
clearly depicting Jupiter enthroned;
Mahomet's profile on a Hershey Bar;
and all Olympus in a blueberry muffin.

Look east, a five-Martini-sunset warms
our backs. Beyond our selves, beyond our booze,
beyond Roy Godbold's silvered and fiery silos,
beyond the arid basin, Cathedral Mountain
rears up to nearly seven thousand feet,
an intrusive mass of tilted Permian limestone,
200,000,000-year-old igneous rock,
crystalline, transient in this final lume.

Home base for viewing Marfa Mystery Lights!,
Thunderbird Motel, Restaurant, Trading Post,
Swimming Pool and access to the Highest
Golf Course in the whole of Texas (9 holes),
Cool Summers, Moderate Winters – see y'all!

Advisable to bring roach killer along;
the restaurant is shut; the pool drained empty.

The Courthouse is flammiferous for Christmas –
$25 will procure a flicker
to honour one whom you love and who is dead.

At Panther junction there's a massive tibia
of a Pterosaur which weighed 70 kilos
and had a 36-foot wingspan (more
than a small jet fighter).

                        In the late Cretaceous,
its shadow darkly traversed the Big Bend floodplain.

Look east, the sun, declining, warms our backs,
blushing the water tower's full, rounded bulk
flesh-pink, rose madder, lilac, Indian red –
like a woman's belly in a Bonnard bath.

The usually neglected Mexican tombs
have been attended-to this Day of the Dead:
each dry dirt plot and the little paths between,
fresh-raked like corduroy; bright new plastic blooms
replace the faded grey ones from last year;
a cross made from two sticks of Yucca is decked
with a pink ribbon; two days past Hallow-e'en,
some *hijo*'s pumpkin has become the head
of a hessian-bean-sack-robed unlikely saint
beside the concrete crucifix of a wrecked
vieja's grave, a sad, symbolic tear
bedewing the gourd's cheek in blue gloss paint.